The Sri Lankan Cookbook

Table of contents

Sri Lankan Culture

Ethnic groups in Sri Lanka

Two population groups dominate in Sri Lanka. About 75% [as of 2012] of the population are Sinhalese, while around 15% of the population are Tamil, making up the largest ethnic minority in Sri Lanka. 11.2% of the Tamil people are indigenous Sri Lankan Tamils. The other 4.2% are Indian Tamils, whose ancestors immigrated to Sri Lanka from South India as plantation workers in the British colonial period. Another minority are the Moors - Tamil-speaking Muslims - with a share of 9.2%, who speak of themselves as descendants of Arab traders. There are also the Malays who immigrated from Indonesia and Malaysia during the colonial period, with about 40,000 inhabitants and the Burgher with 37,000, whose ancestors were European colonists and native women.

Religions in Sri Lanka

Religion plays an integral part in Sri Lanka. 70% of the population and mainly Sinhalese belong to Theravada Buddhism. The Tamils are usually Hindus. There are also Muslims and Christians as minorities.

The role of women

Emancipation is slowly arriving in Sri Lanka. Therefore, very disciplined, reserved behavior by women is still expected. Showing skin too much in public places is not liked and the exchange of too much affection with the partner is not permitted.

Sexual assaults are not uncommon in Sri Lanka, so that it can still be very difficult to ward off assaults as a woman traveling alone.

Sports in Sri Lanka

Sport plays a major role in Sri Lanka. There are many sports in Sri Lanka. Cricket is the most popular sport in Sri Lanka. It was brought to Sri Lanka by the British during the British colonial period. The first games took place in the 19th century. In the 1990s, the national team became a serious threat to win the league title. In 1996 they won the Cricket World Cup for the first time and ever since they have been one of the strongest teams in cricket.

Other sports include rugby union, football and netball. Traditional sports include Kabaddi, Gillidanda, Kili Thadthu. Sri Lanka is also home to two martial arts: Cheena di and Angampora.

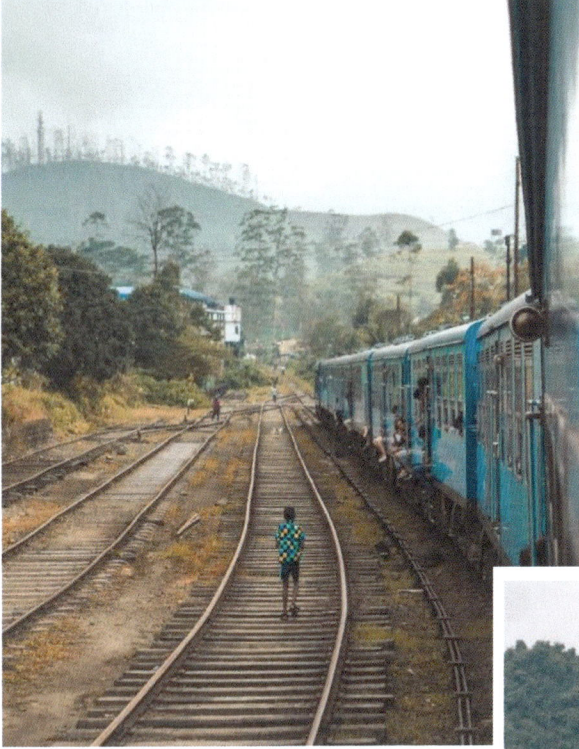

Customs & Traditions

Greeting

To greet someone in Sri Lanka, you fold your hands at head level and bow slightly. As a greeting one says "Ayubowan", which means *May you have a long life*. Shaking hands is unusual in Sri Lanka. If this happens anyway, it should be noted not to use the left hand as it is considered the unclean hand in Sri Lanka. This is due to the fact that the left hand is used for the toilet.

Clothes

Clean and appropriate clothing is expected. Clothes that are too revealing are not welcome at all. In that sense inhabitants don't show their knees or their shoulders. The women in Sri Lanka wear either very long skirts or jeans. The men are - mostly at home, often also on the street - dressed in a so-called Saram in Tamil and Sarama in Sinhalese.

Hospitality

The Sri Lankan proverb *Whatever you do, do it with a smile strongly reflects their motto in life*. Smiling is very important to residents, even in uncomfortable situations. Tourists are treated very friendly, also for economic reasons. Families often invite foreign tourists and show great hospitality and trust in strangers.

Family

In the family, loud laughter and a lot of talking are the norm.

Family is very important. It is particularly important because children are the parents' retirement provision. Married sons stay with their family while married women move in with their husband.

Temple

There are much stricter rules in temples than in the general public. Shoes have to be removed in front of the temple so that you can see a lot of shoes in front of all temples. In addition, you - arms and legs - have to be completely covered. Locals only wear white clothes in temples.

Sri Lankan history

Kingdoms in Sri Lanka

Sri Lanka has been ruled by kings since the third century BC. Under the King Pandukabhaya's rule Anuradhapura became a very powerful kingdom. Buddhism was brought to Sri Lanka in 247 BC by Arahat Mahinda, son of Emperor Asoka of India during the reign of Descendants of Pandukabhaya, King Devanampiya Tissa. Several kings reigned over different capitals. From the beginning of the Christian era to the end of the 4th century AD, Sri Lanka was ruled without interruption by invaders from southern India, which eventually occupied the kingdom of Anuradhapura.

Colonial period

The Portuguese came in 1505 and ruled until 1656 the coastal regions. From 1656 to 1796 the Dutch came to Sri Lanka – who still ruled the coastal regions and could not occupy the whole country – while another sri lankan king ruled in the highlands of Kandy. The Dutch were eventually replaced by the British, who then took over the Kingdom of Kandy in 1815 and occupied the whole island. The British colonial period strongly shaped the country. The infrastructure and cultivation of coffee - subsequently tea - was promoted.
Sri Lanka gained its independence in 1948. In 1972 the new constitution changed the name from *Ceylon* to *Sri Lanka*.

Civil war

The civil war began in 1983 between the Sinhalese government and the opposing Liberation Tigers of Tamil Eelam (LTTE). The Tamils were fighting for the independence of the north. 2002 the government and the Liberation Tigers of Tamil Ealam negotiated ceasefire. Because of still ongoing provocations, the Sri Lankan government decided to end the ceasefire in 1998 and to fight for the liberation of the north. On September 20. 2009 the war ended with the victory of the Singhalese government over the Tamil Tigers. Since then there has officially been peace despite still existing tensions. Sri Lanka has recovered and is increasingly developing into a very touristic country.

The food

In Sri Lanka you eat with your hands. Small balls are formed with the hand which are then pushed into the mouth with the thumb. However, only the right hand is used because the left hand is considered unclean. Sri Lanka's cuisine is one of the spiciest in the world. The hot spices are important because they kill bacteria.
.

Spices and vegetables are a very important part of Sri Lankan cuisine. Vegetarian food is common in Sri Lanka, mainly because many don't eat meat due to their religion. As a result, vegetarians enjoy many varied dishes in Sri Lanka. Locals eat three times warm a day, mostly rice

Recipes

Coconut Roti

In a large bowl, add flour, coconut flakes, water and salt.

Knead the dough until everything is well combined and perfectly smooth.

Let the dough rest for 30 minutes at room temperature.

Turn in you cast- iron skillet on medium heat.

Make 6 – 8 balls from the dough.

Roll out each one into you desired thickness.

Place the roti to cook from each side until it shows brown spots.

Grease with oil as needed.

Remove from heat when cooked.

Serve warm with Coconut Sambol.

2 cups Flour	
1 Cup coconut Flakes	
1/2 Cup Water	
Salt	
Oil (for cooking)	

Coconut Sambol

In a mortar and pestle, add chill flakes, along with salt and sugar.

Grind well until no seed is visible and add in Maldives fish Chips.

Add the coconut flakes and grind well again to get the color of chili paste.

Chop the onion and add in the mixture. Grind well until it forms a paste.

Lastly squeeze in the lemon, mix and serve.

2 cups coconut flakes

2 Tbsp Red Chili Flakes

11/2 Tbsp Maldive Fish Chips

1 medium sized onion

1/2 Tbsp salt

1 Tbsp sugar

1 squeezed lime

Parippu Curry

Wash and boil the lentils with saffron, chili powder, turmeric, curry and cloves.

When the color of lentils is changed to yellow, remove from heat and place it in a large bowl.

Heat oil on medium heat in a large skillet. Fry fenugreek, mustard and cumin seeds for 30 seconds.

Add in garlic and onion and mix well.

Pour in the lentils and mix. Cook well for 5 minutes.

Add in coconut milk and salt to taste. Cook until the curry boils.

Remove from the heat and add in lime juice.

Garnish with hot pepper and serve.

.

Ingredients
1 Cup Red Lentils
2 Cloves, Chopped Garlic
2, Chopped Onions
4, Thinly Sliced Curry Leaves
¼ Tsp Saffron Powder
½ Tsp Curry Powder
½ Tsp Turmeric
½ Tsp Fenugreek Seeds
¼ Tsp Cumin Seeds
1 Tsp Mustard Seeds
½ Tsp Chili Powder
1 Cup Coconut Milk
1¼ Cup Water
2 Tbsp Vegetable Oil
½ Lime
1 Green Hot Pepper
Salt

Pathola Maluwa

Heat oil in saucepan over medium heat, add in curry leaves, thinly sliced pandanus leaf, mustard seeds and green chili pepper for 30 seconds.

Add in the medium, grated onions and fry till translucent. Add in crushed garlic and fry for a bit longer.

Add in all other spices along with, smoked and dried Maldives fish and peeled and cut in halves snake gourd. Mix well and cook for 6 – 8 minutes.

Eventually, add in the lime juice and coconut cream. Now cook for 4 minutes.

Serve warm and enjoy.

Ingredients
2 Tbsp Coconut Oil
½ Tsp Mustard Seeds
6 Curry Leaves
1 Pandanus Leaf
2 Onions
2 Garlic cloves
1 tbsp Maldives Fish
½ Tsp Fenugreek Powder
¼ Tsp Turmeric Powder
¼ Tsp Chili Powder
½ Tsp Curry Powder
Salt
10 oz Snake Gourd
1⅔ Cups Coconut Cream
1 Tsp Lime Juice

Rabu Curry

Heat oil on medium heat, in a pot. Add in Peppers, curry leaves and onions.
Fry for 3 – 5 minutes and stir occasionally.
Add all other spices and mix well.
Add in the radish and cook for 5 minutes.
Lastly, add coconut milk and simmer on low-medium flame for 5 minutes.
Serve hot.

Ingredients
10 Oz. peeled and julienne cut thickly White Radish
1, Sliced Onion
3, Sliced Green Hot Peppers
3, Chopped Curry Leaves
½ Tsp Ground Mustard Powder
½ Tsp Ground Fenugreek Powder
½ Tsp Turmeric Powder
1 Tsp Curry Powder
½ Tsp Ground Cinnamon Powder
2 Tsp Vegetable Oil
1 Cup Coconut Milk
Salt

Kiri Hodi

In a bowl, mix coconut milk along with turmeric powder and keep aside.

Heat oil on medium flame, in a pot. Add in cinnamon sticks, garlic and fenugreek seeds.

Mix well and add in pandanus leafs, green hot pepper and curry leaves.

Add and sauté the onions. Then, add Maldives fish, mix and pour coconut milk. Bring to boil.

Let it simmer for 4 - 6 minutes. Turn off heat and let it cool.

Add lime juice and salt. Discard the pandanus leaves and cinnamon sticks.

Serve while it is warm with Coconut Sambol or string hoppers.

Ingredients
3 Cups Coconut Milk
2 Medium, Chopped Onions
4 Cloves Chopped Garlic
4 cut and sliced thinly Green Hot Peppers
8 Curry Leaves
1½ Tbsp Fenugreek Seeds
3 cut into equal halves Pandanus Leaves
1 Cinnamon Stick
1 Tbsp Turmeric Powder
4 Tbsp Lime Juice
4 Tbsp Vegetable Oil
1½ Tbsp Maldives Fish
Salt

Idiyappam

In a large bowl, add in flour and salt. Knead it with warm water until it becomes soft dough.
Put the dough inside the string hopper press.
Press the string hopper in circular motion onto the string hopper mats or banana leaves.
Place the mats in a steamer of boiling water, over medium heat.
Let it seam for 8 – 10 minutes till it is cooked.
Serve it hot with coconut milk gravy.

2 Cups Rice Flour

2 Tbsp Warm Water

1½ Tbsp Salt

For Equipment:

String Hopper Press

Appam

Mix yeast with water and let it rest for 10 minutes till it activates and foams up.

In a large bowl, add in rice flour, salt and sugar. Stir in the activated yeast, cover and let it set in a warm place for at least 2 hours.

Batter should be thin. Adjust by adding milk if it is thick.

Over medium heat, grease a pan and add in the batter around it, covering the surface.

Cook until the sides are crispy and obtains a brownish color.

Place the Appam onto the plate, serve when warm.

3½ Cups Rice Flour
1 Cup Lukewarm Water
1 Tbsp Active Dry Yeast
2 Cans Coconut Milk
1 Tsp Salt
1 Tbsp Sugar
½ Tsp Baking Soda

Kokis

In a large bowl, beat egg and sugar. Add in turmeric and salt to it and mix well.

Mix in rice flour and coconut cream by hand. Form smooth and creamy mixture.

Over a large wok, heat coconut oil and dip in the Kokis mold until it becomes hot.

Immerse the mold into the mixture and again in oil immediately.

The dough will separate from the mold. Let it cook from both sides.

Place a paper towel on a plate.

Continue cooking the kokis the same way and place in on the plate.

Can be eaten as it is or dipped in honey for sweeter style.

They can be stored in an airtight container up to a week.

Ingredients
1¼ Cups Rice Flour
¾ Cup Coconut Cream
½ Tbsp Turmeric
1 Egg
Coconut Oil for frying
2 Tbsp Sugar
1 Tsp Salt

Lunu Miris

Using a mortar and pestle, crush all the ingredients except the lime juice.

Crush the ingredients well enough to develop the taste.

Add lime juice and salt to taste. Mix well.

Take it out on a plate and serve with fresh lime.

Ingredients
Onion 1 Large, Chopped
1 Tbsp Red Pepper
2 Tbsp Chili Powder
1 Tbsp Maldives Fish
2 Tsp Lime Juice
Salt

Lunu Dehi

In boiling water, add 10 limes for 30 seconds and drain. Wipe and dry each lime.

Cross cut the end of each lime and open those by hand. Stuff kosher salt and close them.

Lay flat the stuffed limes in shallow dish and pour lime juice on them from the remaining limes. Add in 2 pinches of kosher salt.

Place near heat to dry for 48 hours.

Take out the dried limes and cut into quarters. Place in an airtight container.

Add in the remaining juices of the limes and mix in peppers, cardamom and cloves.

Pour in vinegar till all limes are submerged. Shake jar to mix well.

Can be stored in cool dry place, for weeks and is a perfect snack for in-between.

Ingredients
15 Yellow Limes
1 Tsp Red Pepper
2 Tsp Pepper Powder
6 Crushed White Peppercorns
4 Whole Cloves
4 Crushed Pod Cardamom
1 Tsp Sugar
White Vinegar
Kosher Salt

Kiribath (Milk Rice)

Wash and boil the rice along with water and salt. Bring it to boil, uncovered on a medium heat. Eventually, cover it and let it simmer on medium-low heat until all water is absorbed.

Mix in coconut milk and let it simmer on low heat until the coconut milk is absorbed.

Remove from heat and let it cool.

In a deep dish, spread parchment paper and pour the whole mixture.

With a sharp knife, cut it in square shapes and let it solidify for 10 minutes

Take out the pieces in a serving tray and serve.

450 Grams White Short Grain Rice (kekulu)
3 Cups Coconut Milk
5 Cups Water
Salt

Vegetable Roti

In a large bowl, mix flour, salt and water. Make balls from the dough and dip them in oil for 4 hours.

Stir the vegetables along with spices. Mix them in mashed potatoes.

Roll out the dough and add the filling onto it. Fold it and cover from all sides in any shape.

Heat the pan over medium flame and cook all the roti's from all sides till they are golden brown.

Serve warm.

For Dough:

1 Cup Flour
½ Cup Water
1½ Cup Vegetable Oil
Salt

For Filling:

½ lb, boiled and peeled Potatoes
½ lb Leeks
2, Chopped Onions
5, minced Garlic
2 chopped Green Chilies
4 Medium, Grated Carrots
1 inch Pandan Leaf
1 Tbsp Salt
1 Tbsp Pepper Powder
1 Tsp Turmeric Powder
1 Tsp Red Chili Powder
3 Tbsp Vegetable Oil

Kottu Roti

In a non-stick skillet, heat 1 tablespoon oil over medium heat. Add in eggs and mix well till the eggs are scrambled.

In another deep skillet add 2 tablespoon vegetable oil over medium heat. Stir the onions, ginger and garlic. Stir till the onions are translucent. Add in carrots and stir fry.

Mix in cabbage and scallions and all other spices, along with vinegar and soy sauce on low flame.

In the vegetable mixture, add in eggs and roti pieces.

Cook till all the flavors are well combined.

Serve when hot, season with dried herbs.

Ingredients
4, beaten Eggs
1 Medium, Chopped Onion
3 Cloves, Minced Garlic
1 Tbsp Minced Ginger
5 Small, Julienne Cut Carrots
1 Cup, Chopped Cabbage
4, Sliced Scallions
2 Tsp Soy Sauce
1 Tsp Vinegar
3 Cups, Chopped Roti/ Paratha
1 Tsp Turmeric Powder
2 Tbsp Chili Powder
¼ Cup Curry Powder
Salt
Pepper
3 Tbsp Oil

Kaju Aluwa

Coat the rice flour onto a large cutting board.
In a pan, make sugar syrup on medium flame by adding sugar and water. Lower the flame and let it boil for 5 minutes.
Over a large skillet, on medium-low flame, add 2 cups of rice flour and roast it for 5 minutes.
Add the chopped cashews into the readied sugar syrup along with the spices and roasted flour. Mix little at once to have a fluffy dough.
Turn off the heat and place the mixture onto the floured board. Smooth it out on the board at ½ inch thickness, diamond cut.
Take out the shapes and serve.

1 Cup White Sugar
1 Cup Water
2¼ Cups Raw Rice Flour
½ Cup, Chopped Cashews
1 Tsp Fennel Seeds
4, Seeds (Only Cardamom Pods)

Malay Achcharu

Wash the vegetables and let them dry onto a cloth.

The vegetables should be free of moisture.

In a blender, add dates, garlic, mustard seeds, sugar, vinegar, salt and red pepper flakes. Blend into a thick paste.

Place all the vegetables in a large bowl and pour the prepared paste onto it.

Mix everything till it is well combined.

Can be stored in an airtight container for 5 -6 days at room temperature and 11 – 15 days in refrigerator.

Serve with rice.

Ingredients
8 Oz, Peeled Shallots
6 Oz, Cut in large pieces Red Onions
2 Cloves Garlic
5 Oz, Sliced Green/Red Peppers
5 Oz, Julienne Cut Carrots
4, Diced Green Hot Peppers
10 Oz, Pitted Dates
1 Tbsp Sugar
2 Oz. Mustard Seeds
½ Cup Coconut Vinegar
2 Tbsp Red Pepper Flakes
Salt

Ulundu Vadai

Soak the dal for 2.5 hours at room temperature and 30 minutes in refrigerator. Drain.

Blend ginger, peppers and dal together. Add dal little by little along with iced water.

Transfer the dough to a bowl and add all the remaining ingredients to it. Refrigerate for 20 minutes.

Heat oil in skillet and also prepare iced water in a bowl.

Soak hand in the iced water and take the dough in hand, shape it using your thumb to make hole in the center.

Put the dough (vadai) into the hot oil for frying. Re-do to make all vadas.

Fry on medium flame till all sides are golden.

Ingredients
5 oz. split Urad Dal
5, chopped finely Scallions
2 Green Peppers
3 Tbsp Cilantro Leaves
1 Ginger
2 Pinches Asafoetida Powder
Salt
For Frying Oil
Water Iced

Fish Cutlets

In a wok, heat 3 tablespoon oil along with garlic, ginger and cumin seeds for a minute.

Add onions and green chilies to it and fry till onion browns. Add in leeks and sauté.

Add the salt, and other spices along with tuna and mix well.

Add in the boiled potatoes and mash it with other ingredients. Make it smooth and mix in lime juice.

Make small balls of the whole mixture.

In a separate bowl, whisk an egg. Place breadcrumbs in another deep dish.

Dip each ball in the egg then in the crumbs. Set them on a tray.

Heat oil for frying and place each crumbed ball into the oil.

Fry until it turns crisp and golden in color.

Serve hot with ketchup.

Ingredients
150 Grams Tuna Fillet
300g Boiled Potatoes
1 Tbsp Paste Garlic, Ginger
½ Tsp Cumin Seeds
1 Chopped Onions
150 Grams Leeks
2 Chopped Green Chilis
1 Chopped Curry Leave
1 Tsp Red Chili Powder
½ Tsp Turmeric Powder
½ Tbsp Black Pepper Powder
½ Tsp Salt
½ Tsp Lime Juice
3 Tbsp Oil
Oil For Frying
250 Grams Breadcrumbs
2 Eggs

Samosa

In a large bowl, knead stiff dough by adding flour, salt, oil and water. Let it rest for half an hour.

Heat oil in a pan, add garlic, ginger and curry leaves. Fry for a minute then add in leek along with salt and other spices. Stir and fry for another 5 minutes.

Add potatoes and lime juice through the mixture, combine well.

Take out the dough and divide it into 8 parts. Roll them out in a circle and place filling onto them.

Shape them into a triangle to form Samosa.

Fry them in a saucepan until they turn crispy and golden.

Serve hot and enjoy!

Ingredients
300 Grams Flour
1 Tsp Salt
45ml Oil
300g Boiled and Mashed Potatoes
2 Tbsp Oil
5 Curry Leaves
1 Tsp Paste Garlic
1 Tsp Paste Ginger
1 sliced Leek
1 ½ Tbsp Curry Powder
½ Tsp Chili Powder
1 Tsp Salt
100 Grams Peas
1 Juiced Lime
Oil for Frying

Seeni Sambol

Heat Oil in a pan over low flame and add in the chopped onions along with cinnamon, cloves and curry leaves.
Sauté until the onions turn brown in color.
Add tamarind juice, salt, sugar and chili powder.
Cook until the whole mixture turns brown.
Turn off flame after 5 – 7 minutes and let it cool.
Serve with hopers or bread.

250g Chopped Red Onions
1 Tbsp Red Chili
½ Tbsp Sugar
½ Tbsp Tamarind Juice
1 Stick Cinnamon
2 Cloves
2 Cardamom
2 Curry Leaves
2 Tbsp Oil
Salt

Sri Lankan Gold Cake

Grease and line an 8 cm-deep cake pan and preheat the oven to 180°C.

Sift in the flour along with Baking powder in a large bowl.

In another bowl, beat butter and sugar till they are fluffy and well combined. Add in the beaten eggs to it.

Add vanilla and beat again.

Pour this mixture to the flour slowly by folding it in.

Mix well and lay out the mixture onto the greased pan.

Bake for 40 minutes or until it is done.

Let it cool and serve.

250 Grams Flour	
250 Grams Butter	
250 Grams Sugar	
4, Beaten Eggs	
¾ Cup Milk	
1 ½ Tsp Baking Powder	
1 ½ Tsp Vanilla Extract	

Chili Bites

Activate the yeast by adding warm water and let it rest for 10 minutes.

In other cup, mix food color with a bit of water.

In a large bowl, Sift salt and flour. Then, add the yeast and food color to it and knead dough.

Cover and let it rest in a warm place.

After 2 hours, take out the dough and roll it out. With a cookie cutter, shape out the dough in circle with another small hole in the center, obtaining a ring shape.

Heat oil in a wok and start frying till the color is golden brown.

In a bowl add ½ teaspoon salt and red chili powder.

Coat each fried piece into the mixture.

Serve or store in an air tight container.

Ingredients
2 Cups Flour
½ Tsp Sugar
1 Tsp Yeast
50ml Warm Water
1 Tsp Salt
A pinch Orange Food Color
Oil
2 tsp red Chili Powder

Love Cake

Line in a baking dish with butter paper and preheat the oven to 180°C.

In a dry pan, roast the semolina and add butter to it till it melts. Mix well and set aside.

In a large bowl, beat eggs and sugar. Gradually add in all the other spices and ingredients to it.

Also, mix in the semolina mixture in and spread it out in a baking pan.

Bake for 1 hour or till it is done.

Allow the Cake to cool before serving.

Ingredients
1 ½ Cup Semolina
6 Large Eggs
1 ¼ Cup Caster Sugar
4 Tbsp Honey
1 Cup Butter
½ Tsp Almond Extract
3 Tbsp Rose Water
½ Tsp Powdered Cinnamon
½ Tsp Powdered Cardamom
¼ Tsp Powdered Nutmeg
8 Oz Grinded Cashews
3 Oz Diced Winter Melon
1 Tbsp Lime Zest

Thalu Guli

Over low flame, in a dry pan, toast the sesame seeds till they are brown.

Toast the coconut flakes in the same way.

In a mortar, add sesame seeds and salt. Pound for 15 minutes.

Add in the jaggery and crush again. Pound in the toasted coconut. Set aside.

In a non-stick pot, add palm syrup and boil on medium flame for 5 minutes.

Add the syrup to the prepared mixture. Mix with a spoon and then by hand when it is easy to touch.

Make balls from the mixture and fill it with sesame seeds. Place them on parchment paper. Repeat the process.

Serve or stored in an airtight container.

1 ½ Cups White Sesame Seeds
2/3 Cup Grated Jaggery
1 Cup Coconut Flakes
½ Cup Palm Syrup
1 Pinch Salt

Kalu Dodol

Over medium heat, place a shallow pan; add jiggery, rice flour and coconut milk. Bring to boil and stir continuously for about 15 minutes.

Once the mixture is thick, mix in the cardamom and cashews.

After 40 minutes, you will have a jelly like mixture when the oil separates. Fold in the edges to the middle.

Remove the oil once it is fully separated (Approx. after 50 minutes).

Remove as much oil as possible while keep folding in the sides.

Take out the mixture in a tray and set it aside.

Cut into shapes when cooled and serve.

Can be store in an airtight container.

Ingredients
6 Seeds (Crushed) Cardamom Pods
2¼ Cups Coconut Milk
9 Oz Chopped Kittul Jaggery
½ Cup Rice Flour
1 Oz Chopped Cashews

Kaju Maluwa

In a bowl of water, soak the cashews for an hour. Drain and set aside.

In a pan, heat the butter and add garlic, onion, curry leaves, peppers and mix well.

After 4-6 minutes add chili powder all the other spices. Stir for a minute.

Add in the drained cashews and coconut milk. Bring to boil and let it simmer for 15 minutes on low flame.

Add the coconut cream and simmer for another 5 minutes.

Serve hot with rice.

Ingredients
8 Oz Cashews
1 Chopped Onion
5 Cloves Garlic
10 Leaves Curry
2, Chopped Green Peppers
½ Tsp Toast & Crushed Fennel Seeds
½ Tsp Toast & Crushed Cumin Seeds
½ Tsp Turmeric
1 Tsp Chili Powder
¼ Tsp Curry Powder
4 Pods Cardamom
1 Stick Cinnamon
1 Cup Coconut Milk
½ Cup Coconut Cream
2 Tbsp Clarified Butter

Baabath

In cold water, soak the tripe for 4 -6 minutes. Wash well and change water multiple times.

Cut in square shapes and blanch in a large amount of boiling water on high heat for 2 minutes. Drain and dry.

Roast the coriander seeds and then the cumin seeds. Crush them in a mortar.

Sauté the onions in a cast iron pot.

Add in all the ingredients except half the coconut milk. Mix and boil.

Simmer on medium heat for a minute till tripe is tender.

Mix in the remaining coconut milk and let it simmers for 5 minutes. Stir continuously.

Serve and enjoy!

Ingredients
2 Lb Honeycomb Tripe
2 Tsp Cumin Seeds
1 Tsp Powdered Turmeric
3 Curry Leaves
2 Tsp Chili Powder
2 Tsp Coriander Seeds
1 Tsp Ginger Powder
1 Pandanus Leaf
4 Whole Cloves
2 Crushed Lemongrass
6 Cloves Cardamom
1 Stick Cinnamon
1 Large Chopped Onion
3 Cloves Chopped Garlic
1, 2-inch Chopped Ginger
1 Tsp Salt
2 Cups Coconut Milk
1 Juiced Lime
1 Cup Cold Water
3 Tbsp Vegetable Oil

Wattalapan

Preheat the oven to 150°C/300°F.

Over low heat, in a pan, add Coconut Milk, Vanilla and Sugar. Stir continuously for 5 minutes till sugar melts.

Let it cool while stirring time to time.

Beat the eggs till fluffy and whisk into the lukewarm coconut mixture.

Filter it through a sieve.

Divide the mixture into 4 ramekins and place in the oven for 30 minutes. Top it with cashews and back for another 10 minutes.

Remove it from the oven and let it cool down.

Sprinkle with the remaining cashews and serve cold.

Ingredients
Oz Grated Palm Sugar
1 Cup Coconut Milk
¼ Tsp Nutmeg Grounded
1 pinch Grinded Cinnamon
¼ Tsp Cardamom Powder
½ Tsp Vanilla Extract
5 Eggs
1 Oz. Crushed Cashews

Kiri Aluwa

Grease and refrigerate pan square pan with 2 tablespoon butter.

Mix the evaporated milk with water, butter and sugar for 5 minutes.

Cook on medium flame for 20 minutes till the mixture turns brown in color.

Once it begins to thicken, add vanilla, cardamom and cashews. Mix well for 10 – 15 minutes.

Transfer the mixture onto the refrigerated pan. Spread it evenly and pre-cut square shaped pieces.

Let it cool and serve.

Ingredients
1 ½ Cup Evaporated Milk
8 Oz. Caster Sugar
5 Tbsp Butter
¼ Cup Water
2 Oz, Grinded Cashews
1 Tsp Vanilla Extract
2 Pinches Cardamom

Wambatu Moju

Heat oil in a large skillet on medium flame.
Fry the eggplant from both sides till it browns.
Remove from heat and place on paper towels.
Fry onions, peppers and curry leaves in the same oil. Remove and place them on paper towels.
Fry the Maldives Fish in the same oil again till it´s brown and remove from the oil.
Crush ginger and garlic. Also, grind in mustard seeds, coriander, sugar, turmeric, salt and vinegar.
In a large skillet, heat 2 tablespoons of oil over medium flame. Add the fried vegetables, fish and paste. Combine everything.
Sauté for 2 minutes, stirring continuously.
Serve and enjoy.

Ingredients
½ lbs cut in small strips Eggplants
1 large thickly sliced Red Onion
10 Lengthwise cut Green Hot Peppers
10 Curry Leaves
3 Cloves Crushed Garlic
1-inch piece Chopped Ginger
2 Tbsp Maldives Fish
2 Tbsp Chopped Cilantro
1½ Tbsp Mustard Seeds
1 Tbsp Turmeric Powder
3 Tbsp Vinegar
3 Tsp Sugar
Oil for Frying
Salt

Elumas Curry

Wash the meat and Place in a large bowl. Add all the ingredients of marinating and mix by hand till all are combined well.

Marinate for an hour.

In a saucepan, heat oil and add all the spices along with onions till they turn golden.

Add in the marinated meat and mix well.

Cover and boil the meat for an hour or until tender on medium flame.

Add in the coconut cream and let it simmer for 15 minutes till the sauce gets thick.

Remove from heat. Season with spice blend and lime juice.

Mix well and serve.

Ingredients
1½ lbs, Deboned Lamb Shoulder
4 Tbsp Vegetable Oil
½ Tsp Cumin Seeds
½ Tsp Fenugreek Seeds
½ Tsp Mustard Seed
2 Cinnamon Sticks
3 Cardamom Pods
2 Pandanus Leaves
10 Curry Leaves
1 Thinly Sliced Lemon Grass
2 Cut Lengthwise Green Peppers
1 Chopped Onion
2 Cups Boiled Water
1 Cup Coconut Cream
½ Tbsp Sinhalse Curry
½ of Lime Lime Juice
Salt

For marinating

4 cloves, chopped Garlic
1 piece, Chopped Ginger
1 Tablespoon Sinhalese Curry
1 Tablespoon Chili Powder
1 Teaspoon Turmeric
4 Tablespoons Vinegar
2 Teaspoons Salt

Nelum Ala Curry

Instructions	Ingredients
Add fenugreek and mustard seeds into a hot oiled pan till the seeds begin to pop.	1 lb Sliced (Frozen or Fresh) Lotus Roots
Add the onion and sauté. Add lotus root, garlic, spice blend, turmeric, curry and half pandanus leaves.	1 Thinly Sliced Red Onion
	3 Cloves pressed Garlic
Sauté for a minute or two till the spices are well mixed.	1 Tsp Fenugreek Seeds
	3 Tsp Curry Powder
Stir in the milk of coconut and mix for 2 minutes.	1 Tsp Turmeric
Cover and let it simmer till the lotus is tender.	1 Cut in ½ inch pieces Pandanus Leaf
Serve and enjoy.	10 Curry Leaves
	1 Can Light Coconut Milk
	1 Can Thick Coconut Milk
	2 Tbsp Sambal Sauce
	1 Chopped finely Green Chili Pepper

Fish Rolls

In a wok, heat the oil and add garlic, ginger paste and cumin seeds. Then add the onions and green chilies.

Let the onions fry until they are golden brown and add then the tuna. Combine in all the other spices and mix well.

Remove from heat and add boiled onions.

Mix and set aside.

Take readymade roll pastry and spread them out. Add the prepared mixture onto them and fold it in the desired roll shape.

Prepare breadcrumbs in a bowl and beaten egg in another.

Dip the roll first into the eggs and then in the crumbs.

Heat oil in a wok for frying and add the rolls one by one.

Remove when they are crispy.

serve hot with ketchup or another dip.

Ingredients
150g Tuna Fillet
300g Mashed Potatoes
½ Tsp Cumin Seeds
1 Tbsp Paste Garlic Ginger
2 Chopped Onions
2 Chopped Green Chilies
1 Chopped Curry Leaves
1 Tsp Red Chili Powder
½ Teaspoon Turmeric Powder
½ Tablespoon Pepper Powder
½ Teaspoon Salt
3 Tablespoon Oil
Pastry Readymade Roll
250 g Breadcrumbs
2 Beaten Eggs

Fish Puff Pastry

In a wok, heat oil and add garlic, ginger paste and cumin seeds. Add onions and green chilies. Brown the onions and add tuna. Combine in all the other spices and mix well.

Remove from heat and add the boiled onions. Mix and set aside.

Preheat the oven to 200°C/390 F.

Cut the pastry sheets in any shape of your desire.

Place the filling in between and cover it from all sides. Place on baking tray.

Beat egg with 1 Tablespoon water and coat the pastries.

Bake for 15 minutes or till golden brown.

Serve warm and enjoy!

Ingredients
150g Tuna Fillet
300g Mashed Potatoes
½ Tsp Cumin Seeds
1 Tbsp Paste Garlic Ginger
2 Chopped Onions
2 Chopped Green Chilies
1 Chopped Curry Leaves
1 Tsp Red Chili Powder
½ Tsp Turmeric Powder
½ Tbsp Pepper Powder
½ Tsp Salt
3 Tbsp Oil

For Puffs

Ingredients
5 readymade Puff Pastry Sheets
1 Egg
¼ Cup water

Prawn Vada

Let the lentils soak for 2 – 3 hours.
Wash the prawns and set aside.
Grind half the Daal with ginger.
Put it in a bowl and add the remaining Daal and all the other herbs and spices and mix well.
Heat oil for frying in a wok.
Take out the mixture and form a ball. Press one prawn into it.
And cover it with the mixture.
Put it in oil and fry till it´s golden in color.
Remove onto a paper towel.
Serve hot with ketchup.

Ingredients
1 Cup Split Red Lentils / Masoor Daal
250g Small and Unshelled Prawns
2 Chopped Onions
3 Chopped Green Chili
3 In small pieces, crushed Red Chili
1 Inch Ginger
1 Chopped Curry Leaves
¼ Bunch Coriander Leaves (Fresh)
1 Tsp Cumin Seeds
1 Tsp Fennel Seeds
½ Tsp Salt
Oil For Frying

Chicken Curry

In a large bowl, marinate chicken with curry powder, salt and pepper. Set aside.

In a wok, Heat the coconut oil and add all the herbs and spices along with onions, except coconut milk. Sauté for 7 – 8 minutes.

Add in the chicken in the wok and cook. Cover and let it simmer for 10 – 15 minutes.

Cook till the sauce is thick and the chicken is tender.

Serve warm with Sambol or Roti.

Ingredients
6 (600g) Chicken Thigh Fillets
2 Tablespoons Vinegar
60 Grams Curry Powder
1 Tsp Salt
1 Tsp Powdered Black Pepper
2 Tbsp Coconut Oil
1 Sliced Onion
2 Diced Chili Pepper
10 Green Cardamom
6 whole Cloves
12 Curry Leaves
1 Tsp Ginger Paste
2 Cinnamon Sticks
4 Diced Garlic Cloves
1 Large Diced Tomato
2 Tbsp Curry Powder
200 Ml Coconut Milk

Sago Coconut Cookies

Preheat the oven to 150°C/300 F.

In a large bowl mix coconut, breadcrumbs, fennel seeds, coconut and salt.

Add in a bit water if the mixture is dry.

Grease a baking tray and make cookie shapes out of this mixture.

Bake for 40 minutes or till they have a brown color.

Serve straightaway or store in an airtight jar.

Ingredients
125 Grams Sago
125 Grams Coconut Flakes
125 Grams Sugar
125 Grams Breadcrumbs
1 Teaspoon Fennel Seeds
1 Pinch Salt

Point Pedro Vadai

Soak the Daal for 3 – 4 hours and drain.
Then add in a large bowl the Daal along with all the other ingredients and knead dough using boiled water. Use a bit of oil to avoid stickiness.
Make small balls in flatten it on the palm.
Heat oil for frying in a wok.
Fry the prepared Vadas when oil is ready.
Fry in batches till color turns golden.
Drain on paper towel.
Serve when hot with a cup of tea.

Ingredients
125g Broken Urad Daal
300 Grams Roasted Rice Flour
2 Tbsp Red Chili Powder
¼ Tsp Turmeric Powder
¼ Tsp Crushed Broken Chili
3 Cloves grinded Garlic
1 Medium Chopped Onion
1 Chopped Curry Leaves
1 ½ Tbsp Cumin Seeds
Salt
Boiled Water
Oil For Frying

Mushroom Masala

In a pan, heat oil and add mustard seeds, cumin and fennel seeds till they splutter. Then, add the cinnamon stick.

Add in the onions, pandan leaves, curry leaves and green chilies.

Sauté untill the onions are brown. Then, add the tomatoes and mushrooms.

Cook for a minute or two and add red chilies, turmeric, salt and coriander. Mix in curry powder and garam masala.

Cook for 15 – 20 minutes or until the mushrooms are soft.

Add sugar and cook for another 5 minutes.

Remove from heat and garnish with coriander leaves.

Serve and enjoy!

Ingredients
250g Sliced Mushroom
2 Sliced Onion
1 Sliced Tomato
1 Spring Curry Leaves
1 Broken Pandan Leaves
3 Sliced Green Chili
1 Tsp Garlic Paste
½ Tbsp Ginger Paste
½ Tsp Mustard Seeds
1 TspCumin Seeds
1 Tsp Fennel Seeds
1 Cinnamon Stick
1 Tsp Red Chili Powder
2 Tsp Coriander Powder
½ Tsp Turmeric Powder
1 Tsp Salt
1 Tsp Curry Powder
½ Tsp Garam Masala
¼ Chopped Coriander Leaves
2 Tbsp Cooking Oil

Chili Pineapple

Peel the pineapple and cut into chunks.
Put in in skewers.
Mix the spices and sprinkle it over the pineapples.
Allow to rest for 15 minutes and serve.

1 Ripe Pineapple
1 Tsp Red Chili Powder
1 Tsp Black Pepper Powder
½ Tsp Sugar
1 Tsp Salt

Coconut Tapicona

Boil tapioca with turmeric and salt.
Peel and cut in cubes.
In a pan, heat oil and add Urad Daal along with mustard seeds
Add curry leaves, dry chili and onions when mustard seeds splutter.
Fry until the onions are brown.
Add the tapioca and mix for a minute.
Stir in the coconut flakes.
Serve warm.

Ingredients
200g, Cubed Tapioca Boiled
1, Sliced Onion
1, Dried Red Chili
1 Sprig Curry Leaves
½ Tsp Mustard Seeds
½ Tsp Urad Daal
½ Teaspoon Salt
½ Tsp Turmeric Powder
2 Tbsp Coconut Flakes

Chickpea Sundal

In a pan, heat oil and add red chili, coconut pieces, Urad Daal and mustard seeds.
Add in the boiled chickpeas and mix.
Ready to be served as a snack.

1 Cup Chickpeas Boiled	
½ Tsp Mustard Seeds	
1 Tsp Urad Daal	
2 Tbsp Coconut Pieces	
3 Pieced Dry Red Chili	
1 Tsp Salt	
½ Tbsp Oil	

Sri Lankan Kisses

Preheat the oven to 150°C and set parchment paper into a tray.

In a large bowl, whisk the eggs with an electric beater.

Continue to whisk till they become white and fluffy, with stiff peaks.

Add in the tartar cream along with sugar and whisk again.

Add the vanilla extract and pinch salt.

Whisk till it forms the consistency of a smooth, thick batter.

In a large piping bag having star tip, fill in the mixture.

Pipe the kisses onto the baking tray. Then put it in the oven with opened door for 5 minutes and then closed for 15 – 18 minutes or till they are done.

It should be hollow when lifted.

Switch off the oven and let them cool in the oven for 2 – 2.5 hours (don't close the oven door).

Take them out and serve!

Ingredients
4 Egg Whites
250 Grams Sugar
¼ Tsp Cream of Tartar
1 Tsp Vanilla Extract
1 Pinch Salt

Beetroot Coconut Salad

In a pan, over medium low heat, add beetroots, onion, turmeric, garlic, green chilies and all other spices except coconut.

Add water to it and cook till the beetroots are tender.

When the water is reduced, add in oil and fry the beetroot.

Lower the heat. Add coconut. Cook well.

Serve warm with any dish.

Ingredients
250g Thin slices Beetroot
½ Tsp Turmeric
1 Medium Sliced Onions
2 Split Green Chilies
3 Cloves Sliced Garlic
½ Cup Water
1 Tsp Red Chili Flakes
2 Tbsp Oil
1 Cup Coconut Flakes
Salt

Adai

Soak the rice and lentils overnight.
Grind them all into a paste.
Add in red chilies and funnel seeds to the grinder and grind well.
Pour the mixture in a large bowl and add water if required.
Add in the curry leaves, ground chilies, onions, asafetida and salt.
Mix the whole mixture well.
Heat a pan and pour in the batter a ladleful.
Grease oil over it.
Let it cook till both sides are brown.
Serve warm and enjoy.

¼ Cup Urad Daal
¾ Cup Channa Daal
3 Tbsp Toor Daal
¼ Cup White Rice
1 Chopped Onion
1 Chopped Curry Leaves
4 – 5 Red Chilies
2 Tbsp Funnel Seeds
¼ Tsp Asafoetida
Salt

Kithul Treacle Gingersnaps

Preheat the oven to 180°C/350 F and prepare a baking tray using parchment paper.

In a large bowl, sift flour, baking soda, salt, ginger powder and cinnamon.

In another bowl, cream butter, sugar and treacle together.

Beat in the egg as well and fold in the mixture to the flour mixture.

Mix well and then using a scoop spoon, take out spoonful of the mixture and set onto the baking tray. Bake for 20 minutes or till done.

Allow to be cooled before taking them out in a plate.

Serve and enjoy!

250 Grams Flour
150 Grams Butter
200 Grams Brown Sugar
¼ Cup Kithul Treacle
1 Eggs
1 Tbsp Ginger Powder
2 Tsp Baking Soda
1 Tsp Salt
¼ Tsp Cinnamon

Rava Kesari

In a pan, heat 1 Tablespoons of ghee and toast semolina.
Add in 2 cups of hot boiling water and mix well. Don't let the mixture lump.
Once the semolina is cooked, add in 2 cups of sugar and mix well.
Pour in the food color, cardamom powder and remaining ghee.
In another pan heat 1 Tablespoon of ghee and add in the cashews till they are brown.
Mix the cashews in the semolina mixture.
Cook until the mixture starts to separate from the pan.
Put it in a deep dish and cut into any shape.
Serve warm.

Ingredients
1 Cup Semolina
2 Cups Sugar
2 Cups Water
1 Tsp Cardamom Powder
¼ Cup Ghee
10, Chopped Cashews
1/8 Tsp Orange Food Color

Kesel Muwa

Refill the banana blossom bottle with fresh water and set aside for 15 minutes.

Drain water. Collect the flowers after peeling the petals. Chop them finely.

In ½ cup water, Mix salt and turmeric powder. Add the chopped flowers as well and let it rest for 15 minutes.

Over medium flame, heat the wok with oil and add spluttered mustard seeds.

Add in the Urad Daal, cumin seeds, curry leaves, onions, garlic and chilies. Sauté till onions are brown.

Drain the banana blossom and add in the wok.

Then, add salt and turmeric and mix for 3 minutes.

Now add in water and cook well till they tender.

To the end add in the coconut flakes and mix.

Serve hot with rice and enjoy!

Ingredients
300 Grams Banana Blossom (Fresh or pickled)
1 Medium Chopped Onion
2 Pods Minced Garlic
1 Sprig Curry Leave
3 Dry Broken in Pieces Red Chilies
½ Tsp Mustard Seeds
½ Tsp Urad Daal
¼ Tsp Turmeric Powder
½ Tsp Cumin Seeds
4 Tbsp Coconut Flakes
½ Tbsp Oil
¼ Cup Water
Salt

Printed in Great Britain
by Amazon